Caius

Reasons to W

Writing Across the Curr

EDCO *Aidan Herron, Anne Marie Herron, Jane Kelly, Dolores O'Donnell*

Contents

Recount Writing

In this kind of writing, we

★ tell about things that have happened to us or others.

★ tell about the events in the order in which they happened.

★ tell about **who** was there, **what** happened, **when** it happened, **where** it happened and **why** it happened in that way.

★ say what we thought about the events.

Recount writing is found in

★ Storybooks
★ Diaries
★ Newspapers
★ Letters and emails
★ History books
★ Eye-witness accounts

When writing recounts, it helps to

★ think about interesting topics.

★ find various ways to present recounts, e.g. email, websites, letters, articles.

★ make sure that the sequence or chronological order of events is accurate.

★ choose interesting words and phrases to describe events.

★ say in conclusion what you think about these events.

An Email

In this email to her pen pal, Rachel recounts what her class did for a school in South Africa.

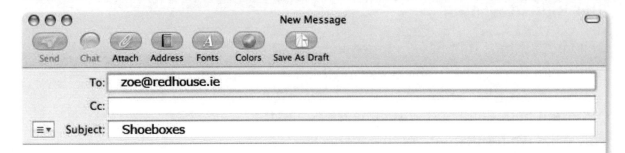

New Message

Send   Chat   Attach   Address   Fonts   Colors   Save As Draft

To: zoe@redhouse.ie

Cc:

Subject: Shoeboxes

Hi Zoe,

I must tell you about an amazing project our class has been involved in. It all started in September when Ms O'Connor told us all about her holidays in South Africa. She told us about a small country school called Mpondweni School near Spion Kop in KwaZulu Natal. There were no proper facilities, no running water, no electricity, no heating, not even proper tables and chairs. She said that the children seemed sad. We were sad too thinking about them because we are so lucky here in our school. So we decided there and then that we would help to make life a bit easier for those children. Ms O'Connor suggested that we could start by sending some small gifts and that's what we did.

Over the next few weeks we gathered shoeboxes and filled them with all sorts of treats, both interesting and funny. We put in small toys and hair bands, pencils, gloves, copies, warm socks — in fact anything we thought the children would like. We filled the boxes until they were brimming to the top with goodies. We wrapped them in brightly coloured paper and wrote the children's names on them. On 1 October the boxes were placed in a huge container and sent by sea, air and train from Dublin to Spion Kop. We tracked the journey on the Internet so we knew that the shipment arrived at Mpondweni School exactly a week later.

On 15 October we received a letter from the teacher in South Africa. She enclosed photos of the children in her school opening their presents. We could see that they were very excited and thrilled to have a present of their own for the first time in their lives. The children also sent us beautiful drawings which we displayed in our school.

The shoeboxes were such a great success that we wanted to help a little bit more. So after Christmas the whole school started to fund-raise so that each child in Mpondweni will have a tracksuit to wear to school, keeping them nice and cosy during their winter months of July and August. We are going to send drawings as well so that they can decorate their school as we decorated ours.

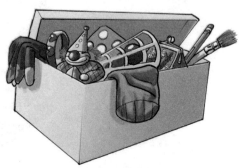

Maybe your school might try to do something like this? It has been great fun and we've made new friends in another country.

I will see you soon.

Rachel

Examine Rachel's Email

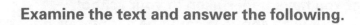

Examine the text and answer the following.

(1) What is the subject matter of this email?

_____

(2) What place is it about? _____

(3) Who are the people mentioned? _____

_____

(4) Why did Rachel's class decide to help?

_____

(5) Write in sequence the events of this friendship project.

In September _____

_____

On 1 October _____

_____

On 8 October _____

_____

On 15 October _____

_____

After Christmas _____

_____

In July/August _____

_____

_____

(6) What items would you include in a shoebox for a child in a school with limited resources?

_____

_____

(7) Locate KwaZulu Natal on a map of South Africa.

3

Write an Email about a Project

Write an email recounting a project you have undertaken in your school. Discuss with your class what you could write about. It could be a fund-raising event, a music or art competition, a Green Schools campaign or something that you have done to help others.

○ ○ ○   New Message   ⊖

Send   Chat   Attach   Address   Fonts   Colors   Save As Draft

To: _____

Cc: _____

☰▼   Subject: _____

Hi _____

Name the project. _____

I want to tell you about _____

_____

Who was involved? _____

_____

Why was the project undertaken? Give reasons.

_____

_____

_____

Write the sequence of events during the project.

Dates	Sequence of Events

Results of the project – Conclusion

_____

_____

_____

Revise and check this first draft. Write the final draft in your copy or on your computer.

Grammar and Punctuation (1)

Sentences

> **Remember!**
>
> A sentence must have a **subject** and a **verb**.
>
> **Example:** The dog barked.
>
> **dog** is the **subject**.   **barked** is the **verb**.

(A) Underline the subject and circle the verb in the following sentences.

1) The baby sleeps.   2) Her friend won.   3) The team lost.

> **Remember!**
>
> Most sentences have a **subject**, a **verb** and an **object**.
>
> **Example:** Our cat drinks milk every day.
>
> **milk** is the object.

(B) Circle the object in the following sentences.

1) The postman opened the gate.   2) She watched the programme.

(C) Using three different coloured highlighters, markers or pencils, underline the subject, verb and object in the following sentences.

1) The gardener tended the plant.   2) He cooked a casserole for dinner.

> **Remember!**
>
> A sentence with one idea is a **simple** or **one-clause sentence**.
>
> **Example:** We wrapped the presents.

(D) Pretend that you are a pupil in Ms O'Connor's class who took part in the fund-raising for the tracksuits. Write four more simple or one-clause sentences about what your class did to raise funds.

1) The teacher organised a monster raffle.

2) _____

3) _____

4) _____

5) _____

Special Olympics 2003 – Opening Ceremony

The opening ceremony of the Special Olympics 2003 took place in Croke Park. This diary recount of the event was written by one of the 30,000 volunteers who attended the ceremony.

21 June 2003

I felt really privileged to be in Croke Park this evening to share in the celebrations of the achievements of more than 7,000 athletes from 150 countries. This was the first time that the games were held outside the United States and it is the largest sporting event in the world this year. The ceremony promised to be a spectacular occasion, with the stadium packed to capacity. RTÉ broadcast the event live to a worldwide audience of millions of viewers.

First, we found our seats high up in the Hogan Stand and waited for the ceremony to begin. The audience had been provided with flags of various colours. We all practised a Mexican wave, using the flags to form a sea of colour around the stadium. Then it was time for the ceremony to begin, with an official opening by President Mary McAleese.

The spectacle began with a 'Dash of Colour'. Representatives of the Host Towns took part in an energetic, fast-moving dance routine and then formed a guard of honour for the participating delegations as they paraded around the grounds. This was followed by 'The Ball', a performance directed by theatre group Macnas and inspired by the various games in the Olympics in which balls are used. Performers dressed in colourful and playful costumes burst into the stadium from all directions. People were stunned by the arrival of the Ball Boy, a giant twenty-metre-tall inflatable character.

After this the largest Riverdance troupe of over 100 dancers entertained with their amazingly skilled display of Irish dancing. Then the arrival of the Special Olympics flag was heralded by 150 drummers playing in unison.

'Solstice' came next. This was a performance which celebrated the fact that the event was happening on the longest day of the year.

The entertainment continued with the appearance of an array of stars including U2, The Corrs and Arnold Schwarzenegger.

The culmination of the ceremony came when the Special Olympics Torch, the flame of hope, having been carried in relay around Europe, was used to light the Games Flame. Once the flame was lit, an amazing display of fireworks exploded in the Dublin sky. Then Nelson Mandela closed the ceremony by declaring the games open for eight days of competition. We left the stadium with the Special Olympics anthem, 'May We Never Have to Say Goodbye', ringing in our ears. It had indeed been a wonderful and moving occasion and the memory will stay with us for a long time.

Examine the Diary Entry

Examine the recount of the Special Olympics Ceremony and answer the following.

1. What major event is described in this recount?

   _____

2. Who participated in the event?

   _____

3. Where and when did it take place?

   _____

4. Why was it an important occasion?

   _____

   _____

5. Explain the following words.

   spectacular _____

   capacity _____

   heralded _____

   solstice _____

6. Choose six highlights of the ceremony and in your copy write a sentence for each, placing the events in sequence.

7. Write six words or phrases which capture the atmosphere of the ceremony.

   _____   _____   _____

   _____   _____   _____

8. Use the Internet to find out more about the Special Olympics movement and its work for people with disability. (Use the Internet only under adult supervision.) In your copy, write ten facts that you have discovered about the Special Olympics in Ireland.

Write a Diary Entry

Write about a show or a sporting event that you attended. Try to capture the excitement and atmosphere of the occasion. Use descriptive words and phrases. Make sure to sequence the events in the correct order.

Name the occasion/spectacle. _____

On **what date** did it take place? _____

Where did it take place? _____

Who attended? **Who** participated in it? _____

_____

Describe the occasion, sequencing the events in the order in which they happened.

Event 1

_____

_____

_____

Event 2

_____

_____

_____

Event 3

_____

_____

_____

Event 4

_____

_____

_____

In conclusion, say what you thought about the occasion that you have described.

_____

_____

_____

Revise and check this first draft. Write the final draft in your copy or on your computer.

Grammar and Punctuation (2)

More about Sentences

> **Remember!**
>
> When **simple** or **one-clause sentences** are joined together with **link words**, the new sentence is called a **compound sentence**.
>
> Each clause is complete on its own.
>
> **Example:** Joe could not play football **because** he was injured.
>
> **because** is the link word joining up the two clauses.
>
> Link words are called **conjunctions**.
>
> **Examples: and, so, as, unless, until, but, because, although, if**

(A) Underline the clauses in each of the following sentences from 'Special Olympics 2003 — Opening Ceremony', and circle the conjunctions.

    1) This was the first time that the games were held outside the United States and it is the largest sporting event in the world this year.

    2) It had indeed been a wonderful and moving occasion and the memory will stay with us for a long time.

> **Remember!**
>
> Sentences with more than one clause are sometimes **complex sentences**.
>
> The **main clause** makes sense on its own, but the other clause does not.
>
> **Example:** After she had got her pocket-money,
>
> Joanne bought a book.
>
> **'Joanne bought a book'** is the **main clause**.
>
> It makes sense on its own.
>
> **'After she had got her pocket-money'**
> This does not make sense on its own.

(B) Underline the main clause in each of the following complex sentences from 'Special Olympics 2003 — Opening Ceremony'.

    1) Once the flame was lit, an amazing display of fireworks exploded in the Dublin sky.

    2) This was a performance which celebrated the fact that the event was happening on the longest day of the year.

(C) In your copy, write an example of another compound and another complex sentence from 'Special Olympics 2003 — Opening Ceremony'.

Guide Dogs

Irish Guide Dogs for the Blind puts its dogs through a training programme. The organisation's website describes the life of these wonderful animals from birth to retirement. See http://www.guidedogs.ie. This recount was written using this website for information. Use the Internet only under the supervision of an adult.

First Steps

Cloud began his life with his mother in the home of a volunteer boarding family. The family made sure that he was safe, healthy and warm. At five weeks old, he was brought to the Training Centre to see if he was suitable for Guide Dog work. Cloud had the right temperament and was accepted.

Early Learning

At six weeks, he was placed with a volunteer Puppy Walker called Laura who house-trained him, groomed him and taught him to be obedient to commands. Laura trained Cloud to be confident and happy in a variety of settings by walking him on busy streets, on country roads, in shops and railway stations, on lifts and escalators, and by travelling with him on buses and trains. The pup learned to cope with heavy traffic, roadworks and loud noises. He even learned how to behave in churches and restaurants.

Off to School

When Cloud was a year old, he left Laura and her family to join forty other dogs at the Training Centre. Here he spent five months with a specially trained instructor, doing what is called 'early training'. Each day he went on several walks, learning how to cross roads, stop at kerbs and avoid obstacles.

Cloud then went on to 'advanced training' where his skills were perfected so that he would be able to provide safe mobility for a blind or visually impaired person.

When Cloud was twenty months, he was chosen to be a guide dog for a man called Harry. Together they attended classes for three weeks at the Training Centre in Cork. There they got used to each other's ways and learned to work together. Harry and Cloud got on very well together and became great companions. Cloud was always loyal, caring and watchful, helping Harry to get around in safety. Harry has always appreciated Cloud and relied on him to do many daily tasks.

Retirement

Now, after ten years, Cloud is getting tired and has just retired from his job as Guide Dog. Harry will soon be given a new dog but he will keep Cloud as a pet, allowing him to rest after a life's work well done.

Examine the Text

Examine the text and answer the following.

(1) List the four stages in the life of a guide dog.

_____

_____

_____

_____

(2) Explain: temperament _____

mobility _____

visually impaired _____

appreciated _____

(3) Why was Cloud seen to be suitable for training as a guide dog?

_____

_____

(4) What happens during early training?

_____

_____

_____

(5) What extra skills does the dog learn during advanced training?

_____

_____

_____

(6) Write four facts that you learned about guide dogs.

_____

_____

_____

_____

(7) What do you think are the most important skills that a dog needs to be
a good guide dog? _____

_____

_____

_____

Write about a Racehorse

With your class, research how racehorses are trained. Recount the life story of a racehorse.

When was the horse born? _____

Where was it kept at first? _____

Who looked after it? _____

_____

In this frame, write about what happened to the horse.

When it was young _____

_____

_____

When it got older _____

_____

_____

What kind of training was it given at first?

_____

_____

_____

What advanced training did it receive?

_____

_____

_____

What were its achievements, e.g. races?

_____

_____

_____

When did it retire and where was it looked after?

_____

_____

Revise and check this first draft. Write the final draft in your copy or on your computer.

Persuasive Writing

In this kind of writing, we

★ give our point of view.

★ show different points of view.

★ argue a case.

★ try to persuade our readers.

★ come to conclusions.

Persuasive writing is found

★ on Internet sites.

★ in debates.

★ in book and film reviews.

★ in advertising.

★ in newspaper articles.

★ in brochures and leaflets.

When you write to persuade, it helps to

★ think about how to present different points of view.

★ study examples of persuasive writing in advertisements, articles, etc.

★ choose words that will attract attention and convince.

★ present your work in a way that will capture the reader's interest, e.g. add illustrations and photographs.

An Internet Site

Internet sites can give us very useful information and advice. They can persuade us to change something or improve our lifestyle as this one does: http://www.healthysteps.ie. Use the Internet only under the supervision of an adult.

Take Five Steps to a Healthier You

Step 1 – Physical Activity

Physical activity should be part of growing up for young people. Physical activity includes play, games, physical education, sport, walking, cycling, dancing and lots more besides!

Young people should be physically active in order to

- achieve physical fitness and stay healthy and well.
- develop active lifestyles which will last through their lives.
- reduce the risk of serious disease in adulthood.

The benefits of physical activity:

- It helps to build strong bones, healthy joints and a healthy heart.
- It promotes a good state of mind.
- With a balanced healthy diet, it will maintain a healthy weight.
- It makes you feel good.
- It helps you to make friends.
- It's fun!

Children and young people need to do at least one hour of moderate-intensity activity most days of the week. This means that you will start to feel warm. Your heart rate will increase and your breathing will be heavier but you will still be comfortable talking.

Top ten tips to get active

- Put on some music and dance.
- Walk to the shops, to school or to after-school activities.
- Play outside. Play chasing, hopscotch, skipping and ball games.
- Spend less time watching TV and playing video games.
- Join a club and learn a new skill, e.g. swimming, football, karate, basketball.
- Go for walks with your family.
- Fly a kite in your local park.
- Play a number of sports, not just one.
- At the weekend, go for a walk, cycle or swim.
- Join a local summer camp or sports club.

Examine the Website

Read the text from the Internet site. Discuss it with your class and answer the following.

1. Why do children and young people need to be active?

   _____

   _____

   _____

2. Read on page 14 the list of benefits of physical activity.

   Number them 1–6 in what you think is their order of importance.

3. Write out the three that would persuade **you** to get active.

   _____

   _____

   _____

4. Read the explanation of 'moderate-intensity'. Think of six activities that would make you feel this way.

   _____   _____

   _____   _____

   _____   _____

5. Read the **Top ten tips to get active**. Then, with your class, think of other ways to keep fit. Make a list to pin up on the classroom notice board.

   Our Top Ten Tips

   _____   _____

   _____   _____

   _____   _____

   _____   _____

   _____   _____

6. Page 14 deals with just one step to a healthier you. List four other steps that you could take.

   _____

   _____

   _____

   _____

Design an Internet Information Site

Design an Internet information site to persuade children to eat more fruit and vegetables.

○○○

◄ ► C + ⊖   ⊙ ⌃

»

Eat Your Greens!

(A) List three reasons why children need to eat more fruit and vegetables.

_____

_____

_____

(B) Suggest some delicious and/or unusual fruit and vegetables which children could try.

Fruit	Vegetables
_____	_____	_____	_____
_____	_____	_____	_____
_____	_____	_____	_____
_____	_____	_____	_____

(C) Write ten top tips to encourage children to eat more fruit and vegetables.

Top Ten Tips

1) Put an apple in your lunch box every day.

2) _____

3) _____

4) _____

5) _____

6) _____

7) _____

8) _____

9) _____

10) _____

Revise and check this first draft. Write the final draft in your copy or on your computer.

Follow-up Activity

In your copy, write a recipe for a healthy snack, incorporating some of your chosen fruit and vegetables.

Grammar and Punctuation (3)

Verbs

(A) Only one of the following is the correct definition of a verb. Write the correct one.

1) the name of a person, animal, place or thing
2) a describing word
3) an action word
4) a word used instead of a noun

A verb is _____

(B) Find four verbs in 'Top ten tips to get active' and write them in the spaces.

1) _____ 2) _____ 3) _____ 4) _____

Remember!

To use a different form of a verb, we often add **ing**.

When we add **ing** to verbs, we sometimes just add **ing**.

Example: think + ing = thinking

When the verb ends with **e**, we drop the **e** and add **ing**.

Example: joke - e + ing = joking

When the verb has one vowel before a single final consonant, we double the consonant and add **ing**.

Example: begin + n + ing = beginning

(C) Complete this table by adding **ing** to the verbs.

run _____	walk _____	sit _____
swim _____	refuse _____	admit _____
start _____	take _____	travel _____
slip _____	shout _____	drive _____
live _____	hop _____	hope _____
chat _____	skate _____	bounce _____

(D) There are eleven verbs ending in **ing** on page 14. Write them below.

_____ _____

_____ _____

_____ _____

_____ _____

_____ _____

_____

A Debate

The topic for debate is 'Greeting cards have had their day'. Lily argues against this in her speech.

I disagree that greeting cards have had their day. In fact, I think that they are still very important.

The custom of sending Christmas cards by post began in 1840 and people have enjoyed sending and receiving them ever since. And no wonder! There is nothing nicer than seeing a card addressed to you dropping through your letter box. You know that someone has been thinking of you and wants to say thank you or is wishing you well on special occasions. You will probably even recognise the handwriting and, before you open the envelope, know who has sent it.

Choosing the right card for a friend is good fun too as there is such a huge variety of cards available for every occasion. Cards come in all shapes and sizes. They can be funny, pretty, musical, artistic and photographic. You can also make and design your own cards for a really personal touch. Some people enjoy handcrafting cards, decorating them with odds and ends to make them more interesting. Blank cards are useful too if you need to write a special message to someone.

Of course, you may think that sending cards is too much trouble as you have to buy stamps and go to the post box. Yes, it can be troublesome but I think that we *should* make an effort for our friends and family. We *should* spend time finding just the right card to suit their personality or to share in how they are feeling. A card carefully chosen will give them great pleasure.

Our opposing team will say that text messages and emails can do the same job but I don't think so. Text messages are short and snappy but somehow they don't have the same appeal. After all, you won't keep a birthday text message for years and years. You won't put it in a frame because it looks so pretty. You won't put it in a box in your attic to look at when you are older, to remind you of people who loved you.

The same is true of emails. Yes, of course photographs and messages can be added to emails, but then you must print them off if you want to keep them. It's just not the same as the noise of a card coming through your letter box just for you. So keep posting those cards and make your friends feel special.

Examine Lily's Speech

Examine the speech, discuss it with your class and answer the following.

(1) Is Lily speaking for or against the motion 'Greeting cards have had their day'?

_____

(2) What in her second paragraph tells you that Lily likes to receive cards?

_____

(3) Why, in Lily's opinion, can choosing cards be fun?

_____

_____

(4) List the occasions for which people might send and receive cards.

_____   _____   _____

_____   _____   _____

_____   _____   _____

_____   _____   _____

(5) Lily guesses what the opposing team will say. What argument does she expect from the opposition?

_____

_____

(6) Why, in her opinion, is it better to receive a card than a text message or an email?

_____

_____

_____

_____

(7) Write other reasons why it is better to receive cards than text messages.

_____

_____

_____

(8) Were you persuaded by Lily's argument about greeting cards? _____ Say why.

_____

_____

Write a Speech

Prepare a speech on the topic 'Video games are bad for children'. You can be for or against.

Opening statement – Say whether you agree or disagree with the statement.

I _____

Give reasons why you take this view.

_____

_____

_____

_____

_____

_____

Give an example of what the opposing team will say.

_____

_____

_____

_____

Now write an answer to this argument.

_____

_____

_____

_____

Write your **concluding argument** to persuade everybody that your view is the right one.

_____

_____

_____

_____

Revise and check this first draft. Write the final draft in your copy or on your computer. When you have completed your speech, read it to the class. Have a class debate. Some people will be for the topic and others against.

Grammar and Punctuation (4)

Adjectives

(A) **Only one of the following is the correct definition of an adjective. Write the correct one.**

1) a word that tells us more about a verb

2) a word that describes a noun or a pronoun

3) an action word

4) a word used instead of a noun

An adjective is _____

> ### Remember!
>
> Some adjectives are formed from nouns or verbs.
>
> **Examples:**   **birthday** party
>
>   **swimming** pool
>
> A number or colour can be used as an adjective.
>
> **Examples:**   **two** apples
>
>   a **red** coat
>
> Adjectives are not always beside the noun or pronoun.
>
> **Example:** The programme was **long** but **interesting**.

(B) **Circle the adjectives that describe the underlined nouns and pronouns.**

1) Grandad read a bedtime <u>story</u> for my little <u>sister</u>.

2) <u>They</u> are happy because they won twenty <u>euro</u>.

3) The racing <u>bikes</u> were punctured, so we went for a two-mile <u>walk</u>.

4) I watched a television <u>programme</u> about a famous <u>explorer</u>.

(C) **What two adjectives are used in Lily's debate to describe text messages?**

_____   _____

(D) **There are nine adjectives used to describe cards in the first three paragraphs of the debate. Write them.**

1)_____   2)_____   3)_____

4)_____   5)_____   6)_____

7)_____   8)_____   9)_____

(E) **Think of three adjectives you would use to describe**

★ greeting cards   _____ _____ _____

★ text messages   _____ _____ _____

★ emails   _____ _____ _____

A Film Review

When we read a good review of a film, we are sometimes persuaded to go to see the film. This review is about the film *Happy Feet*.

Happy Feet is an animated musical comedy that will delight children and charm grown-ups. It tells the story of Mumble, a penguin who is an outcast because he is not like the other penguins who value song above all else. Mumble can do a great tap-dancing routine but when he tries to sing, the others just laugh at him. Mocked and ridiculed, he sets off on an epic journey to discover his heart-song, the key to finding a mate. He wanders alone across the icy wastes of the Antarctic and on his way he meets real danger from gulls and leopard seals, and encounters some 'aliens'. The story is not just a simple heart-warming tale. It looks at the issues of good and evil but also includes messages about the preservation of our environment, which we all should heed.

However, it is the computer animation that makes this a great film. The director and his team have created a believable icy landscape, home to thousands of penguins. The birds themselves are irresistible with their sturdy waddle, their glossy feathers and expressive eyes. A star-studded cast provides the voices of the various characters, and the penguins come to life thanks to some very good performances. Elijah Wood is excellent as Mumble and Robin Williams is hilarious as Ramon.

Many of the computerised sequences are superb. The scene where the penguins swim in formation giving an underwater acrobatic display is unforgettable. As bubbles trail out behind them, we are transported into their surroundings of blue icy seas and natural beauty.

This is an enchanting film and will entertain people of all ages. Best of all, you will come out of the cinema with your feet tapping to the music of your own heart-song. You will enjoy every minute of this magical film.

Examine the Film Review

Read the review and answer the following.

① According to the reviewer, who would enjoy this film?

_____

_____

② Write four sentences to say what this story is about.

_____

_____

_____

_____

_____

③ Write a sentence that praises the computer animation in this film.

_____

_____

④ Find six words or phrases in the text which would persuade you to watch this film.

_____   _____

_____   _____

_____   _____

⑤ Underline the words that best describe the attitude of this reviewer.

positive	undecided	disappointed	delighted	interested
amazed	complimentary	insulting	excited	negative

⑥ The reviewer enjoyed the film and thought that it was worth seeing. Write as many words or phrases as you can, which a critic might use in praise of a film or book.

excellent _____   _____   _____

_____   _____   _____

_____   _____   _____

_____   _____   _____

Write a Film Review

Think about a film that you have seen in the cinema or on DVD. Write a review to persuade your friends to watch it.

Name of the film: _____

Who is it suitable for? _____

Outline the plot of the story. *(Don't reveal the ending.)*

_____

_____

_____

_____

_____

_____

Who directed the film? _____

Who starred in the film? _____

_____

Say something about the way the story was filmed, e.g. setting, scenery,

lighting, costumes, animation, special effects. _____

_____

_____

_____

_____

_____

Describe your favourite part of the film. _____

_____

_____

_____

Say why you would recommend this film. _____

_____

_____

_____

Revise and check this first draft. Write the final draft in your copy or on your computer.

Narrative Writing

We write narratives to entertain the reader with

★ Stories
★ Poems and ballads
★ Fairy tales
★ Folk tales
★ Legends and myths
★ Fables
★ Plays

We find narrative writing in

★ Picture books
★ Storybooks
★ Short-story collections
★ Film scripts
★ Novels
★ Poetry anthologies
★ Comics and graphic novels

When you write narrative, it helps to

★ switch on your imagination.
★ choose carefully what you want to write about.
★ ask yourself who you are writing for.
★ choose a setting and characters for your story.
★ decide on your plot and how it works out.
★ make a plan to organise your ideas.

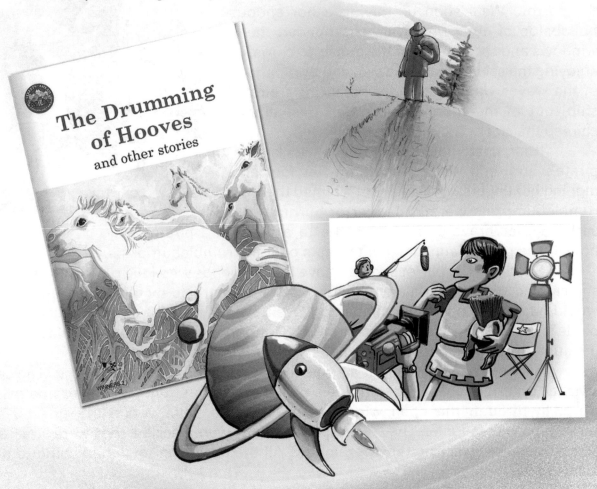

The Horrendous Hullabaloo

There was once a cheerful old woman who kept house for her nephew, Peregrine – a pirate by profession. Every morning she put on her pirate pinafore, picked up Peregrine's socks, and petted his parrot. She worked day in, day out, keeping everything shipshape. Meanwhile, her pirate nephew went out to parties every night, though he never once asked his aunt or his parrot if they would like to go with him.

Whenever his aunt suggested that she and the parrot might want to come too, Peregrine replied, 'You wouldn't enjoy pirate parties, dear aunt. The hullabaloo is horrendous!' 'But I like horrendous hullabaloos!' exclaimed the aunt. 'And so does the parrot.' 'When I come home from sea I want a break from the parrot,' said Peregrine, looking proud and piratical. 'And if I took my aunt to a party, all the other pirates would laugh at me.' 'Very well,' thought his aunt, 'I shall have a party of my own.'

Without further ado she sent out masses of invitations written in gold ink. Then she baked batch after batch of delicious rumblebumpkins while the parrot hung upside down on a pot plant, clacking its beak greedily.

No sooner had Peregrine set off that evening on another night's hullabaloo than his aunt, shutting the door behind him, peeled off her pirate pinafore and put on her patchwork party dress. 'Half past seven!' she called to the parrot. 'We'll soon be having a horrendous hullabaloo of our own!' Then she opened the windows and sat waiting for the guests to come, enjoying the salty scent of the sea, and the sound of the waves washing around Peregrine's pirate ship, out in the moonlit bay. 'Half past eight!' chimed the clock. The pirate's aunt waited.

'Half past nine!' chimed the clock. The pirate's aunt still waited, shuffling her feet and tapping her fingers. 'Half past ten!' chimed the clock. The rumblebumpkins were in danger of burning. No one, it seemed, was brave enough to come to a party at a pirate's house. The pirate's aunt shed bitter tears over the rumblebumpkins.

Suddenly the parrot spoke. 'I have lots of friends who love rumblebumpkins,' she cackled. 'Friends who aren't put in a panic or petrified by pirates – friends who would happily help with a hullabaloo!' 'Well, what are you waiting for?' cried the pirate's aunt. 'Go and fetch them at once!' Out of the window the parrot flew, while the aunt mopped up her tears and patted powder on her nose.

Almost at once the night air was filled with flapping and fluttering. The sea swished and sighed. The night breeze smelled of passion fruit, pineapples and palm trees. In through the open windows tumbled the patchwork party guests, all screeching with laughter. They were speckled, they were freckled; they were streaked and striped like rollicking rags of rainbow. All the parrots in town had come to the aunt's party.

'Come one, come all!' the aunt cried happily. The parrots cackled loudly, breaking into a bit of a sing-song. So loud was the sing-song that the pirate's neighbours rushed out of their houses, prepared for the worst. 'What a horrendous hullabaloo!' they cried in amazement. The aunt invited them all to feast richly on her rumblebumpkins, and to join her in a wild jig. She was having a wonderful time.

When Peregrine arrived home later that night, his house was still ringing with leftover echoes of a horrendous hullabaloo. The air smelled strongly of rumblebumpkins, and the floor was covered in parrot feathers. 'Aunt!' he called, crossly. 'Come and tidy up at once.'

But there was no one at home for, at that very moment, his aunt, still wearing her patchwork party dress, was stealing away on Peregrine's own pirate ship. Over the moonlit sea she was sailing, with parrots perched all over her, making a horrendous hullabaloo. As they sailed off in search of passion fruit, pineapples and palm trees, it was impossible to tell where the aunt left off and the parrots began.

So, left on his own, with a grunt and a groan Peregrine put on the pirate pinafore and tidied up for himself.

by Margaret Mahy

Examine the Story

Read the story and answer the following.

1   Write a sentence to summarise what the story is about. _____
_____
_____

2   What is the source of conflict between the two main characters?
_____
_____

3   How do both characters grow and change in the story?
_____
_____

4   A writer uses *alliteration* when he or she chooses to repeat the same letter or
sound. Underline the places in this story where you find **alliteration**.
How does this help the story? _____
_____

5   For what age group, do you think, was the story written? _____ Why?
_____

6   Is there a moral or lesson for the reader? _____ If yes, what is it?
_____

Plan a Cautionary Tale

Write a cautionary tale, where a character is taught a lesson for being selfish. Write it for younger children who enjoy repetition, nonsense words and rhyme. Discuss other things young children enjoy in a story. Use the frame to make notes.

1) What characters will be in the story? Include describing words.

_____
_____
_____
_____
_____
_____
_____

2) When and where will it take place? Include a description.

_____
_____
_____
_____
_____
_____
_____

3) How will the tale begin?

_____
_____
_____
_____
_____
_____
_____

4) In what way will the character be selfish and how will this affect the other characters?

_____
_____
_____
_____
_____
_____

5) What will the other characters decide to do and how will it all work out?

_____
_____
_____
_____
_____
_____

6) How will everyone feel in the end?

_____
_____
_____
_____
_____
_____
_____

In your copy, write a first draft of your tale. Include some realistic dialogue to help the story along. Write the final draft in your copy or on your computer. Add pictures and make a picture book. Then share it with a younger child.

Grammar and Punctuation (5)

Nouns – Gender of Nouns

> **Remember!**
>
> Nouns may be classified according to **gender**.
>
> Nouns which refer to **females** are **feminine**.
>
> **Example:** mother
>
> Nouns which refer to **males** are **masculine**.
>
> **Example:** father
>
> Nouns that may be **male** or **female** are **common**. **Example:** child
>
> The names of things **without** life are **neuter**. **Example:** bicycle

A   **Put these nouns into the correct column.**

doctor	grandfather	television	school	queen	car	husband	teacher
daughter	nurse	floor	cow	pupil	children	bride	uncle
man	stone	cousin	train	groom	sister	brother	girl

masculine (m)	feminine (f)	common (c)	neuter (n)

B   **Indicate the gender of each of the highlighted words in the following extracts from 'The Horrendous Hullabaloo', e.g. woman (f).**

1) There was once a cheerful old woman who kept house for her nephew, Peregrine – a pirate by profession.

2) 'I have lots of friends who love rumblebumpkins.'

3) Out of the window the parrot flew, while the aunt mopped up her tears and patted powder on her nose.

4) So loud was the sing-song that the pirate's neighbours....

_____ _____ _____

_____ _____ _____

_____ _____ _____

_____ _____ _____

The Arrival of a Stranger

In this extract, the writer introduces a new character into the story. He describes the character in great detail to awaken the reader's interest. Read the extract from the novel and talk about it.

Then a moving figure caught Jody's eye. A man walked slowly over the brow of the hill, on the road from Salinas, and he was headed towards the house. Jody stood up and moved down towards the house too, for if someone was coming, he wanted to be there to see. By the time the boy had got to the house the walking man was only halfway down the road, a lean man, very straight in the shoulders.

Jody could tell he was old because his heels struck the ground with hard jerks. As he approached nearer, Jody saw that he was dressed in blue jeans and in a coat of the same material. He wore clodhopper shoes and an old flat-brimmed Stetson hat. Over his shoulders he carried a gunny sack, lumpy and full. In a few moments he had trudged close enough so that his face could be seen. And his face was as dark as dried beef. A moustache, blue-white against the dark skin, hovered over his mouth, and his hair was white, too, where it showed at his neck. The skin of his face had shrunk back against the skull until it defined bone, not flesh, and made the nose and chin seem sharp and fragile. The eyes were large and deep and dark, with eyelids stretched tightly over them. Irises and pupils were one, and very black, but the eyeballs were brown. There were no wrinkles in the face at all. This old man wore a blue denim coat buttoned to the throat with brass buttons, as all men do who wear no shirts. Out of the sleeves came strong bony wrists and hands gnarled and knotted and hard as peach branches. The nails were flat and blunt and shiny.

The old man drew close to the gate and swung down his sack when he confronted Jody. His lips fluttered a little and a soft impersonal voice came from between them.

'Do you live here?' Jody was embarrassed. He turned and looked at the house, and he turned back and looked towards the barn where his father and Billy Buck were.

'Yes,' he said, when no help came from either direction.

'I have come back,' the old man said. 'I am Gitano, and I have come back.'

Extract from The Red Pony *by John Steinbeck*

Examine the Text

Read the story and answer the following.

1. From whose point of view is the story told? _____ How do you know?

   _____

   _____

2. Which sentence tells you that Jody was curious about the stranger?

   _____

   _____

3. Underline the adjectives on page 30 which are used to extend these nouns in the story.

   > man   jeans   shoes   hat   sack   moustache   chin   eyes   wrists

   How do they help the reader? _____

   _____

   _____

   _____

4. Which sentence makes the reader want to know more about the man?

   _____

5. Having examined the extract closely, make detailed notes about the character.

Physical Appearance	**Clothes**

6. In your copy, sketch a portrait of the old man, including as many details from the passage as possible.

Plan a Character

A writer needs to think about what his or her characters look like, how they are dressed, what they would say or do in different situations, how they feel inside and the effect they have on others.

Choose a character from the list below or invent one. Develop a character profile using the frame.

- a famous actor
- a prima ballerina
- a shy giant
- an angry postman
- an unhelpful shop assistant
- an unhappy frog
- a skilled sculptor
- a talkative bus driver
- a quarrelsome child

Character Profile

My character's name: _____

Physical appearance (Sketch a portrait)	What he/she wears	Things he/she says	

Things he/she does	How he/she feels inside	What the other characters think of him/her	What I think of him/her

Use your notes to write a first draft of your character description. Edit and check that you have described all aspects of your character. Share profiles with your classmates. Write the final draft in your copy or on your computer.

Grammar and Punctuation (6)

Adverbs

A **Only one of the following is the correct definition of an adverb. Write the correct one.**

1) a word that describes a noun

2) the name of a person, animal, place or thing

3) a word that tells us more about a verb

4) a word used instead of a noun

An adverb is _____

Remember!

Adverbs can tell us **when**, **where** and **how** actions are carried out.

Examples: ★ Susan's cat went missing **yesterday**.

yesterday is an adverb. It tells us **when** the cat went missing.

★ She searched **everywhere** for the missing cat.

everywhere is an adverb. It tells us **where** she searched.

★ She searched the garden **carefully**.

carefully is an adverb. It tells us **how** she searched.

B **Write a sentence for each of the following adverbs.**

often   quickly   outside   frequently   forwards

1) _____

2) _____

3) _____

4) _____

5) _____

C **Circle the adverbs in the following extracts from 'The Arrival of a Stranger' and say if they tell us when, where or how the actions were carried out.**

1) A man walked slowly....   _____

2) As he approached nearer, Jody saw....   _____

3) In a few moments he had trudged close enough.... _____

4) ..., with eyelids stretched tightly over them.   _____

5) His lips fluttered a little....   _____

The Sleeping Room

Sometimes a setting helps to create the mood of a story and to prepare us for some event or twist in the story plot. This unusual setting is unfamiliar to the characters in the story and what they find here changes their lives forever. Read the extract and talk about it.

Once they stepped into the room they became aware of a dim blue light and at the same time the door swung silently closed and clicked shut behind them. The blue light seemed to be seeping up through the floor and out of the walls and down from the ceiling. It was a soft, warm, gentle light – rather like the morning sky on a summer's day. Once they got over the surprise and shock, Fionnuala and Aedh looked around in amazement. They had almost expected the room to be dark and dusty like the corridor, but it was sparkling, bright and clean.

The room was round and the walls, floor and ceiling were coloured in different shades of blue. Pictures of sea creatures had been painted on the walls in perfect detail and in glowing colours, and where the walls joined the floor there were more pictures, but this time of sea plants with long waving fronds, multi-coloured flowers and brightly coloured crabs and lobsters. The ceiling had been painted in such a way that it looked like the surface of the water seen from underneath, and for a moment the children were fooled into thinking that they were actually under water, and they felt the air rush in through the sides of their throats as their gills opened.

A door suddenly opened in the wall just in front of them, and blue-green light streamed into the room. A tall figure stepped into the doorway, sending a dark shadow dancing across the floor and up the wall. Fionnuala and Aedh took a few steps back until the strange being ahead of them raised one of its arms and the light died down, and they recognised their father. They ran to him and he hugged them both close.

Extract from The Children of Lir *by Michael Scott*

Examine the Story Setting

Read the extract and answer the following.

1. What happens to create suspense in the very first sentence?

   _____

   _____

2. How do you know that the children had never been in the room before?

   _____

   _____

3. What was the room designed to look like? _____

   What tells us that the children felt that it was very realistic?

   _____

   _____

4. Good descriptions speak to our senses. Find descriptions in the passage to match the following.

   Sight _____

   Hearing _____

   Touch _____

5. How does the use of light and shadow add to the atmosphere of the story?

   _____

   _____

6. Make a sketch of the blue room as *you* imagine it. Use coloured pencils to achieve the watery feel.

Create a Mysterious Setting

Writers and film directors need to create imaginative settings to tell a story. Choose a setting from the suggestions below or invent one of your own. Then draw and make notes for a detailed description, using the frame to help you.

- an enchanted forest
- an alien spacecraft
- an underground home
- an unknown planet
- an underwater cave
- a jungle village
- a haunted library
- a bandit's den
- a sunken ship

Location and time	Physical details – shape, size, furniture and other objects

Atmosphere and mood/lighting	How does the place make you feel?

Choose a good opening sentence and write a first draft of your description. Remember to use your senses to help you to describe. Share your first draft with your partner or group. Write the final draft in your copy or on your computer.

Poetry Writing

In this kind of writing, we

★ select a topic.
★ choose words and phrases carefully.
★ use describing words.
★ sometimes use rhyming words.
★ use words to make a picture or tell a story.

When you write poetry, it helps to

★ think deeply about your subject.
★ use your senses.
★ choose your words carefully.
★ select rhyming words if you like them.
★ use images and metaphors.
★ make a picture with words.

Poetry is found in

★ Poetry anthologies
★ Collections of nursery rhymes
★ Children's stories
★ Songbooks

A Pocketful of Poems
Poetry Anthology 6

A Descriptive Poem

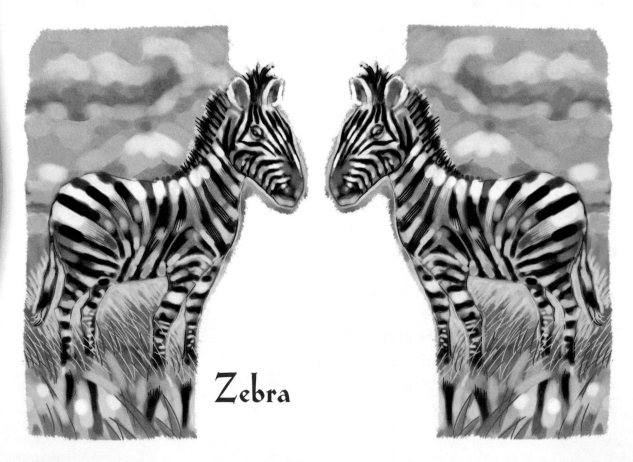

Zebra

People have lost interest in the zebra
since the coming of the colour television.

At the Serengeti waterhole
he dips his ancient heraldic head,
fills his round belly.

On the dry dust of the plain
he casts a blue shadow.
His heavy eyes watch the acacia trees
for the least sign of movement.
He shakes his mane,
the dark plume of a Roman centurion.

At home we take the zebra for granted,
let him carry us across the road
outside the supermarket.

by Gilroy Fisher

Examine the Poem

Read the poem 'Zebra' and answer the following.

1. Use a dictionary to find the meanings of the following words.

    heraldic   _____

    acacia   _____

    centurion   _____

2. The poet says that people have lost interest in the zebra since the coming of colour TV. Why, in your opinion, does he say this?_____

    _____

3. How do you know that the poet himself has *not* lost interest in the zebra?

    _____

    _____

4. The poet describes the zebra by painting images in words. Which image do you prefer?   _____

    Say why.   _____

    _____

    _____

5. What lines in the poem tell you that the zebra has to remain alert when drinking at the waterhole?

    _____

    _____

    _____

6. How could colour television help to reawaken interest in the zebra?

    _____

    _____

    _____

7. How has this poem awakened *your* interest in the zebra?

    _____

    _____

    _____

8. In the last three lines of the poem, which zebra does the poet refer to?

    _____

    Why do we take it for granted?

    _____

Write a Poem

Write a poem about an animal that you think is not fully appreciated.
Use the frame to help you.

My chosen animal: _____

(1) Describe the animal.

_____

_____

_____

(2) Why, do you think, is this animal underappreciated?

_____

_____

_____

(3) What makes this animal unique? Why is it special to you?

_____

_____

_____

My first draft – You may choose to use rhyme if you like.

Begin with: People have lost interest in the _____

_____

_____

_____

_____

_____

_____

_____

_____

_____

_____

_____

Revise your poem and write the final draft in your copy or on your computer.

Grammar and Punctuation (7)

Alphabetical Order

A Put these words in alphabetical order.

1) sell   painful   host   straw   alarm   fame   money   dream

_____

2) thank   time   tall   train   type   teach   trust   toast

_____

Remember!

When words begin with the same **two** letters, we must look at the **third** letter to decide on the order.

Example:

badge   band   basket   battery

B Put these words in alphabetical order.

park   panic   page   pastime   paper   palace

_____   _____   _____   _____   _____   _____

C There are five words in the poem 'Zebra' beginning with **c**. Write them in alphabetical order.

_____   _____   _____   _____

Remember!

When words begin with the same **three** letters, we must look at the **fourth** letter to decide on the order.

D There are eight words in the poem 'Zebra' beginning with **h**.

Write them in alphabetical order.

_____   _____   _____   _____

_____   _____   _____   _____

Where I Hail From

You can't get in your jeep
and drive to where I come from.
Not yet anyway, kids.
Where I started my adventure
we led a primitive existence
without laptops, microwaves,
picture phones or video games.

Hard to imagine, I admit:
walking around in nerdish clothes
and an uncool pair of shoes.
But we were happy there
watching our black and white TV,
playing with our non-battery-operated toys,
thinking our old-fashioned thoughts.

It is so many light years away
that I need to scour my ancient brain
for any dimly lit memories of that place.
I get tired just thinking about it.
Every so often I grab a streetlight
and refuse to keep moving.
Not an option.

We all have to move right along.
I pack my bags each morning
for more time travel,
even further away from where I started.
I am so far away now
I can barely see
the galaxy I hail from.

by Julie O'Callaghan

'Where I Hail From' by Julie O'Callaghan, taken from *Something Beginning with P – New Poems from Irish Poets* edited by
Seamus Cashman, The O'Brien Press Ltd.

Examine the Poem

Read the poem 'Where I Hail From' and answer the following.

① What does the poet mean when she says that you can't drive to where she comes from? _____

_____

② Why does the poet say that she had 'a primitive existence'? (You may need to use a dictionary to find the meaning of the word 'primitive'.)

_____

_____

③ What does she say about the clothes she wore when she was young?

_____

_____

④ What else does the poet remember about her childhood?

_____

_____

⑤ Why might the poet compare where she came from to a galaxy she can barely see?

_____

_____

_____

⑥ What does the poet mean when she talks about packing her bags each morning 'for more time travel'? _____

_____

_____

⑦ What things do you use or play with now that may be old-fashioned when you are grown up? _____

_____

_____

Write a Poem

Use the frame to help you to write a poem about being a time traveller.

If I could get into my jeep and time travel, I would go to _____

I would go there because _____

_____

_____

I would meet _____

_____

_____

I would see/hear/smell/taste/touch *(Make notes.)*

_____

_____

_____

_____

_____

The experience would be _____

_____

My first draft

_____

_____

_____

_____

_____

_____

_____

_____

_____

_____

_____

_____

Revise your poem and write the final draft in your copy or on your computer.

Grammar and Punctuation (8)

The Hyphen

> **Remember!**
>
> The hyphen ⊟ is sometimes used to link words or parts of words to make a longer or compound word.
>
> **Examples:**
>
>
>
> hide-and-seek   twenty-two   see-saw

(A) Write the following numbers using the hyphen.

32 _____   45 _____   63 _____

25 _____   73 _____   99 _____

(B) Choose the correct word or words from the box to complete each of the hyphenated words below.

pig	examine	landing	sit	hearted
old	ladder	year	nine	pin

1) cross-_____   2) guinea-_____   3) rope-_____

4) eighty-_____   5) drawing-_____   6) down-_____

7) baby-_____   8) crash-_____   9) two- _____-_____

(C) Put the hyphen between the correct words in the following sentences.

1) The children need to have high protein meals every day.
2) Our team was leading at half time.
3) It is a cold blooded creature with scissors like jaws.
4) The ten year old boys won the two legged race.
5) The thieves were caught red handed by a passer by.
6) The fire engine arrived soon after the fire alarm went off.
7) We were in the waiting room for at least forty five minutes.
8) The double decker bus stopped at the bus stop.
9) It is illegal not to wear your seat belt.

(D) Write a hyphenated word used in the poem 'Where I Hail From'.

_____

THINK CAREFULLY BEFORE READING THIS

This is a bureaucratic poem.
Please sign (in block capitals)
in triplicate upon receipt.
Knock before entering.
Read the instructions carefully
(Do not exceed the stated dose).
Do not park on the nouns.
Do not walk on the consonants.
Do not spit on the vowels.
Do not recite loudly.
Please leave this poem in the
condition in which you find it.
Flush after use, and
DO NOT DO THAT.

by Andrew Darlington

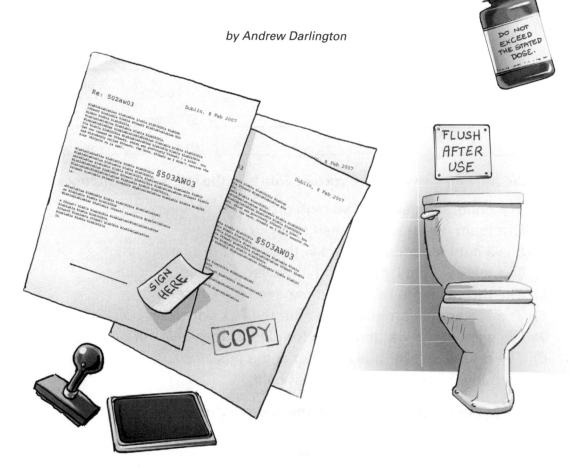

Examine the Poem

Read the poem 'Think Carefully Before Reading This' and answer the following.

1. Find the dictionary meanings of the following words.

   bureaucratic _____

   in triplicate _____

   receipt _____

   exceed _____

   consonant _____

   condition _____

2. In the poem 'Think Carefully Before Reading This', find two instructions that you could easily follow.

   _____

   _____

3. Why, in your opinion, does the writer give instructions that do not make sense?

   _____

   _____

4. Which instruction in the poem is the easiest to obey?

   _____

   _____

5. Write the instruction which you think is the funniest.

   _____

   _____

6. Why, in your opinion, does the poet use brackets for some instructions?
   (Hint – try reading aloud.)

   _____

   _____

7. Do you think that this is a funny poem? _____

   Why? _____

   _____

   _____

Write a Playful Poem

You have just examined a poem where the poet plays with words. Use the frame to help you to write your own playful poem about instructions that you get from adults.

The theme of my poem is 'Things Adults Tell Me Not To Do'

1. Who says 'DO NOT' to you? _____

_____

_____

2. When do you hear 'DO NOT'?

_____

_____

3. Where would you read 'DO NOT'?

_____

_____

4. How do you feel/react when you hear 'DO NOT'?

_____

_____

_____

Give your poem a title and write your first draft below. Start some of the lines with 'Do not' if you wish.

My first draft

_____

_____

_____

_____

_____

_____

_____

_____

_____

_____

_____

Revise your poem and write the final draft in your copy or on your computer.

Report Writing

In report writing, we give information about

★ Objects
★ Places
★ Animals
★ People

Report writing is found in

★ Non-fiction books
★ Newspapers
★ Encyclopaedias
★ Magazines

When you write a report, it helps to

★ know your topic.
★ research the facts.
★ put the facts into categories.
★ think of your audience.

London

Read this report about London.

London, the capital city of England and of the United Kingdom, is built on the River Thames. It is one of the oldest cities in the world and we can trace its history back nearly 2,000 years.

London is a very varied city and its population consists of many cultures, speaking over 300 different languages.

The city is a popular tourist destination, attracting millions of tourists every year. Landmarks such as Big Ben, the London Eye, the Tower of London, the National Art Gallery and Buckingham Palace are amongst its many attractions. Much of London was destroyed by fire in 1666 and again during the Second World War, 1939–1945. Fortunately, after each disaster, most of the old landmarks were rebuilt and there are many interesting sights to visit.

London's busiest shopping areas are Oxford Street, which is nearly two kilometres long, and the Knightsbridge area, which is home to the famous Harrods department store. London is also an international centre of fashion, alongside Paris, Milan, New York and Tokyo.

The area known as 'The City' is the financial centre of London and is home to banks, insurance companies and accountancy firms.

London hosted the Olympic Games in 1908 and 1948 and has been chosen to host them again in 2012. This will make London the first city in the world to host the Olympic Games on three occasions. Well-known annual sports competitions held in London are the Wimbledon Lawn Tennis Championships and the London Marathon in which 35,000 runners attempt a forty-two-kilometre course around the city.

The London Underground transport system, which is the oldest metro system in the world, was built in 1863. Although it is very efficient, traffic is still a problem in London. In 2003, congestion charges were introduced to reduce traffic in the city centre. This means that motorists are required to pay a fee to drive within London's central area.

London is a bustling, exciting city and is home to many of the world's greatest artists, poets, scientists and statesmen.

Examine the Report

Read the text about London and answer the following.

(1) What does the opening sentence tell us about London?

_____

_____

(2) What does the report tell us about the size of London?

_____

_____

(3) Name three of London's tourist attractions.

_____

(4) Where in London would you find Harrods department store?

_____

_____

(5) What is in the area of London known as 'The City'?

_____

_____

(6) How often has London hosted the Olympic Games?

_____

(7) Name two well-known annual sports competitions held in London.

_____

_____

(8) What does the report tell us about the London Underground transport system?

_____

_____

(9) Which area of London would you most like to visit and what would you like to see?

_____

Why? _____

_____

Write a Report

With your group or class, research facts about another city or town. Plan a report about that city or town, using the headings in the frame.

① **Title**

_____

② **Opening sentence or sentences.** *(Say where the city or town is.)*

_____

_____

③ **Describe the city or town.** *(Write facts you have learned from the research, using the following points to help you.)*

★ Size/Population

★ Geographical location

★ History of the town or city

★ Places of historical interest

★ What is special about the town or city

★ Scenic locations

★ Commerce/business in the town or city

★ Annual events/Celebrations

★ Famous people

★ Challenges facing residents

_____

_____

_____

_____

_____

_____

_____

_____

④ **Write a sentence or sentences to end the report.**

_____

_____

_____

Write a first draft. Edit and check your first draft. Write the final draft in your copy or on your computer.

Grammar and Punctuation (9)

Numbers

> **Remember!**
>
> Numbers from **one** to **ninety-nine** are usually written in words.
>
> **Examples:** I bought **two** tickets for the concert.
>
> More than **500** people attended the concert.
>
> For a **mixture** of numbers **above** and **below 100**, both are written as figures.
>
> **Example:** Between 90 and 110 pupils took part in the concert.

(A) **Write the following sentences removing the brackets.**

1) We travelled more than (75) kilometres that afternoon.

2) We bought more than (200) books at the book fair.

3) He painted between (60) and (80) paintings in the last (5) years.

4) The book had between (75) and (130) photographs of animals.

> **Remember!**
>
> Fractions are written in words, e.g. $\frac{1}{2}$ is written as **half**.
>
> Ordinal numbers are written in words, e.g. 1st is written as **first**, 2nd as **second**, etc.
>
> **Example:** About half of our class went to see the concert on the first day.

(B) **Write the following sentences, removing the brackets.**

For more than ($\frac{1}{4}$) of the pupils in the class, it was their (1st) journey on a train.

(C) **Circle where numbers are used in this paragraph from the report on London. Discuss with your partner which rule applies in each case.**

London hosted the Olympic Games in 1908 and 1948 and has been chosen to host them again in 2012. This will make London the first city in the world to host the Olympic Games on three occasions. Well-known annual sports competitions held in London are the Wimbledon Lawn Tennis Championships and the London Marathon in which 35,000 runners attempt a forty-two-kilometre course around the city.

Volcanoes

Talk about what you see in the photographs.

Read this report about volcanoes.

Volcanoes are mountains formed by layers of lava, ash and dust, which erupt from deep within the Earth through openings in the Earth's surface or crust.

There are many different types of volcano. The cinder cone volcano, which is the most common, is rarely more than 400 metres in height and is formed from lava fragments called cinders. The shield volcano is much larger in scale and is formed by multiple layers of lava.

Most of the world's volcanoes are found in and near the Pacific Ocean in an area known as the 'Ring of Fire'. Volcanoes are generally located near coasts and great mountain ranges. There are more than 500 active volcanoes throughout the world and among the best known are Mount Etna and Mount Vesuvius in Italy, Mount St Helens in North America and Mount Fuji in Japan. Many others are said to be sleeping or dormant. Some volcanoes are termed extinct as they have not erupted during the last several thousand years.

When a volcano erupts, magma (red-hot liquid rock), gases and ash are forced through an opening in the Earth's crust. When the magma reaches the surface, it is called lava. Lava is red hot when it erupts, but as it cools, it changes to dark red, grey or black rock.

Volcanoes affect the lives of many people. Houses, buildings and towns can disappear in an instant under a flow of lava. In August AD 79, a volcanic eruption from Mount Vesuvius buried the ancient Italian city of Pompeii and its 20,000 inhabitants. An erupting volcano can trigger tsunamis, flash floods, avalanches, earthquakes and mudflows. In order to prevent disaster, vulcanologists try to determine when volcanoes will erupt, but in many cases volcanoes are unpredictable.

Volcanic eruptions have some benefits. They leave deposits of rich soil, and lava is often used as building material. Pumice stone, which comes from lava, is used for road building and in beauty treatments.

However, volcanoes are spectacular to watch and dramatic when erupting, and they have entranced and fascinated people for centuries. They are a reminder of nature's power and wonder.

Examine the Report

Examine the report and answer the following.

(1) What does the opening sentence tell us about volcanoes?_____

_____

(2) What does the report tell us about

★ the different kinds of volcano? _____

_____

★ the size of volcanoes? _____

_____

(3) Where are most of the world's volcanoes and what is this area known as?

_____

(4) Name three active volcanoes.

_____

_____

(5) Write three other facts about volcanoes that you learned from this report.

_____

_____

_____

_____

(6) What fact about volcanoes did you find the most interesting?

_____

_____

_____

(7) Why, do you think, do people find volcanoes fascinating?

_____

_____

_____

_____

(8) What other natural phenomenon do you find fascinating or spectacular? Say why.

_____

_____

Write a Report

With your group or class, research facts about another of nature's wonders. Write a report using the headings in the frame.

① **Title** _____

② **Opening sentence or sentences** *(Say what it is you are writing a report about.)* _____

_____

_____

③ **Describe this wonder of nature.** *(Write about the facts you learned from the research, using the following points to help you.)*

★ Where and how it occurs

★ How it affects human and natural environments

★ How it is measured or predicted

★ Examples of occurrences

_____   _____

_____   _____

_____   _____

_____   _____

_____   _____

_____   _____

_____   _____

_____   _____

_____   _____

_____   _____

④ **Write a closing sentence or sentences.**

_____

_____

_____

_____

Write a first draft of your report. Edit and check this first draft. Write the final draft in your copy or on your computer.

Grammar and Punctuation (10)

Nouns

(A) Only one of the following is the correct definition of a noun. Write the correct one.

1) a describing word

2) an action word

3) the name of a person, animal, place or thing

4) a word that tells us more about a verb

A noun is _____

(B) Say whether the following statement is true or false.

Proper nouns are written with a capital letter. _____

Underline the proper nouns in this paragraph from the report on volcanoes.

Most of the world's volcanoes are found in and near the Pacific Ocean in an area known as the 'Ring of Fire'. Volcanoes are generally located near coasts and great mountain ranges. There are more than 500 active volcanoes throughout the world and among the best known are Mount Etna and Mount Vesuvius in Italy, Mount St Helens in North America and Mount Fuji in Japan. Many others are said to be sleeping or dormant.

Remember!

To change nouns from **singular** to **plural**, we

- add **s**. **Example:** tree + s = tree**s**
- add **es**. **Example:** bus + es = bus**es**
- change the **y** to **ies**. **Example:** country becomes countr**ies**.
- change the inside of the word. **Example:** man changes to m**e**n.

(C) Look for the plurals of these words in the report and write them here.

1) mountain _____ 2) metre _____ 3) range _____

4) tsunami _____ 5) flash flood _____ 6) avalanche _____

(D) Underline seven plural nouns in these sentences from the report and write their singular.

Volcanic eruptions have some benefits. They leave deposits of rich soil, and lava is often used as building material. Pumice stone, which comes from lava, is used for road building and in beauty treatments.

However, volcanoes are spectacular to watch and dramatic when erupting, and they have entranced and fascinated people for centuries.

1)_____ 2)_____ 3)_____ 4)_____

5)_____ 6)_____ 7)_____

Christopher Reeve

Talk about what you see in the photograph.

Read this report about Christopher Reeve.

Christopher Reeve was a famous American actor. He is probably better known as Superman, the role he played in the *Superman* films.

As a very young boy, Christopher Reeve showed great talent. He excelled in many school activities, including music, sport and drama. By the age of eight, he had appeared in many school plays. Later, Reeve spent time studying theatre in France and England before being accepted into New York's famous Juilliard School of Performing Arts.

Reeve worked in film, television and the theatre. He appeared in a total of seventeen feature films, but he is best remembered for his role as Superman. He hosted and narrated many television documentaries on subjects that were of interest to him, such as stunt work and aviation.

As well as being a successful actor, Reeve was an accomplished pianist and spent several hours a day composing and practising classical music. He was a superb athlete and performed his own stunts in films. He had a pilot's licence and flew solo across the Atlantic Ocean on two occasions. He flew gliders and was an expert sailor, scuba diver and skier. He had a great love of horses and took part in cross-country and show-jumping events.

It was this love of horses that led to the great tragedy in his life. In 1995, he was thrown off his horse during a cross-country event. He had fractured his spine in the fall and was instantly paralysed from the neck down. Reeve now faced life completely dependent on others for his most basic needs.

With the support of his family and close friends, he used his tragedy to help others. He founded the Christopher Reeve Foundation in 1996, to raise money for research and to provide funds to improve the quality of life for people with disability. The millions of dollars raised still help people today.

Christopher Reeve died in October 2004. Many people believe that because of the courage he showed, he was indeed a true 'Superman', and he is remembered with great fondness and admiration.

Examine the Report

Read the report and answer the following.

1. Who was Christopher Reeve? _____
   _____

2. Where did he live? _____

3. Describe his characteristics, skills and talents

   (a) as a young boy.

   _____
   _____
   _____

   (b) as an adult.

   _____
   _____
   _____

   (c) in his later life.

   _____
   _____
   _____

4. Write other facts that you learned about Christopher Reeve.

   _____
   _____
   _____
   _____

5. Why, according to the author, was Reeve a true 'Superman'?

   _____
   _____
   _____

6. What qualities would you attribute to Christopher Reeve, having read this
   account of his life?

   _____
   _____
   _____

Write a Report

Write a report about a person whom you admire. Research facts about this person. Make notes in the frame below, using words and phrases.

① **Title** _____

② **Opening sentence or sentences** *(Who is/was this person?)*

_____
_____
_____

③ **Description**

When and where this person lived/lives

_____

His/Her characteristics, skills, talents, achievements, actions

_____
_____
_____
_____
_____
_____
_____
_____

Other information and interesting facts, e.g. what makes/made this person special

_____
_____
_____
_____
_____

④ **Ending sentence or sentences** *(Include your opinion about this person.)*

_____
_____
_____
_____
_____

Revise and check this first draft. Write the final draft in your copy or on your computer.

Procedural Writing

In this kind of writing, we

★ list sequences of actions.
★ show steps to be taken in doing something.
★ tell how something is done.
★ give instructions on how to operate things.

For procedural writing, it helps to

★ have a clear aim.
★ list what is required.
★ write instructions clearly in a step-by-step way.
★ check that your procedure can be followed.

Procedural writing is found in

★ Cookery books
★ Games, compendiums
★ Assembly kits
★ Science books
★ Route finders

How to Make a Rainmaker

To make a rainmaker, just follow these instructions, step by step. You may need an adult to help you to assemble what you need.

Description: The Rain Maker was a very important person in Native American tribes. During dry periods, he used a tube-like instrument, which made a sound like rainfall sprinkling on the ground, to bring the rain. This percussion instrument is called after him – a rainmaker.

Aim
To make a rainmaker

Materials
★ the inner cardboard tube from tin foil or greaseproof paper
★ cling film
★ rubber bands
★ a drawing-pin (or compass)
★ wooden toothpicks
★ scissors
★ glue
★ dried peas
★ coloured paper

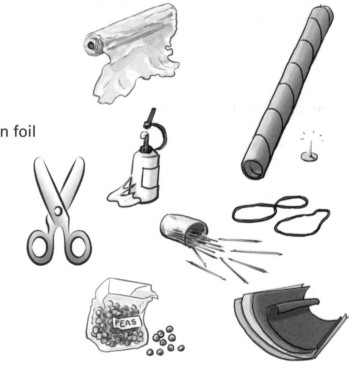

Instructions
1. First, put the cling film over one end of the tube, securing it with a rubber band.
2. Poke about 100 holes all over the tube, using the drawing-pin or compass. (Don't put any holes in yourself!)
3. Push a toothpick into each hole until most of it is inside.
4. Cut off any sharp part of the toothpick that sticks out.
5. Glue around the toothpicks to make sure that they don't fall out.
6. Pour in a cupful of the dried peas.
7. Now put cling film over the other end and secure it with a rubber band.
8. Use the coloured paper to decorate your rainmaker.

Assessment: Tilt the rainmaker slowly from end to end to hear the rain falling.

Examine the Instructions

Examine the text and answer the following.

(1) What is the aim of these instructions?

_____

(2) What was the original reason for using a rainmaker?

_____

_____

(3) Put these steps in the right order:

★ Pour in the dried peas. ★ Decorate your rainmaker. ★ Push in toothpicks.

(a)_____

(b)_____

(c)_____

(4) Why do you need the following?

(a) rubber bands _____

(b) drawing-pin or compass _____

(c) toothpicks _____

(5) What prevents the dried peas from falling out of the tube?

_____

(6) Why should you cut off the sharp ends of the toothpicks?

_____

_____

(7) The sound of a rainmaker is like _____

_____

_____

(8) A rainmaker is a percussion instrument. Name three others.

(a) _____ (b) _____ (c) _____

(9) What alternative materials could you use to make a rainmaker?

_____ _____ _____

_____ _____ _____

Make a Percussion Instrument

Now draw up your own list of instructions for making a percussion instrument. Use the frame to help you.

Making a _____

Description

_____

Aim

_____

Materials   **Illustration**

_____

_____

_____

_____

_____

_____

Instructions

Number the steps.

_____

_____

_____

_____

_____

_____

_____

_____

_____

_____

_____

_____

Revise and check this first draft. Write the final draft in your copy or on your computer. Include diagrams or pictures.

Grammar and Punctuation (11)

Prepositions

(A) **Only one of the following is the correct definition of a preposition. Write the correct one.**

1) an action word

2) a describing word

3) a word that tells you the position of a person or thing

4) the name of a person, animal, place or thing

5) a word that tells us more about a verb

A preposition is _____

(B) **Circle the prepositions among the words in the box. Choose six and write each of them in a sentence.**

decide	into	underneath	pupil	beside	to
across	over	towards	round	basket	by
spent	upon	lonely		through	against	all

1) _____

2) _____

3) _____

4) _____

5) _____

6) _____

(C) **Circle the prepositions in the following sentences from 'How to Make a Rainmaker' on page 62.**

1. First, put the cling film over one end of the tube, securing it with a rubber band.
2. Poke about 100 holes all over the tube, using the drawing-pin or compass. (Don't put any holes in yourself!)
3. Push a toothpick into each hole until most of it is inside.
4. Cut off any sharp part of the toothpick that sticks out.
5. Glue around the toothpicks to make sure that they don't fall out.
6. Pour in a cupful of the dried peas.
7. Now put cling film over the other end and secure it with a rubber band.
8. Use the coloured paper to decorate your rainmaker.

How to Assemble a Stool

To assemble the stool, just follow the instructions below.

Description

A stool is a handy item of furniture, used as seating in kitchens, cafés and classrooms.

Aim

To make a stool

Materials

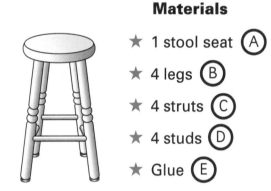

* ★ 1 stool seat (A)
* ★ 4 legs (B)
* ★ 4 struts (C)
* ★ 4 studs (D)
* ★ Glue (E)

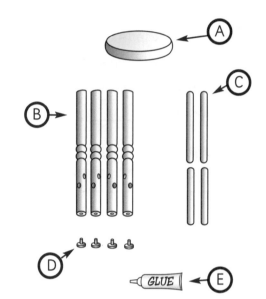

You will also need a wooden mallet.

Instructions

1. Before assembling, place all the parts on the floor.
2. Place the stool seat on the floor upside down.
3. Pour glue into the four prepared holes on the reverse side of the seat.
4. Push the legs fully into the holes. ①
5. Pour glue into the prepared holes in each leg of the stool.
6. Insert the struts into the holes and secure the legs together. Make sure that the struts go in the whole way. ②
7. Tap the legs to ensure that they are now fully secure in the base of the seat.
8. Hammer a stud into the bottom of each leg. Wait for the glue to dry. ③

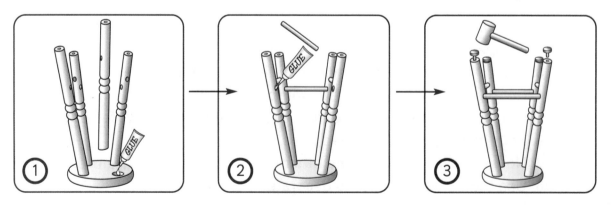

Examine the Instructions

Read the instructions on how to assemble a stool and answer the following.

1. Why is it a good idea to lay all of the materials on the floor before beginning to assemble the stool?

   _____

   _____

2. What is the purpose of illustrating the instructions?

   _____

   _____

3. Why does the stool come with holes already provided?

   _____

   _____

4. What is the purpose of putting studs in the bottom of each leg?

   _____

   _____

5. List two advantages that a stool has over a chair?

   (a) _____

   (b) _____

6. List two advantages and two disadvantages of buying furniture that you have to assemble yourself.

   Advantages

   (a) _____

   (b) _____

   Disadvantages

   (a) _____

   (b) _____

7. List other types of self-assembly furniture.

   _____   _____   _____

   _____   _____   _____

Assemble a Mug Stand

Now write a list of instructions for making a mug stand. Use the frame to help you. Illustrate the materials and instructions.

Making a _____

Description
A mug stand is _____

Aim

_____

Materials | **Illustration**

★ (A) 1 mug-stand base

★ (B) 1 central pole

★ (C) 6 branches

★ (D) glue

Instructions

1.

2.

3.

4.

Revise and check this first draft. Write the final draft in your copy or on your computer.

Grammar and Punctuation (12)

More about Numbers

> **Remember!**
> When using numbers in a list, we write them as numerals.
> **Example:**

Shopping List
6 oranges
4 bananas
6 eggs...

A What numbers are used in the list of materials for 'How to Assemble a Stool' on page 66?

_____

B Using numerals, write a shopping list for a special occasion in your house.

Shopping List for _____

_____ _____ _____
_____ _____ _____
_____ _____ _____
_____ _____ _____

C Design a recipe leaflet for healthy sandwiches for four people, including one vegetarian sandwich. List the ingredients and illustrate the sandwiches.

How to Make a Scrapbook

People who keep scrapbooks are called 'scrappers'. The following instructions for selecting, arranging and decorating material for your Life Scrapbook will allow you to become a scrapper.

Making Your Own Life Scrapbook

Description
Become a scrapper — how to make your own Life Scrapbook

Materials
★   a loose-leaf ring binder
★   a set of cardboard dividers
★   markers, crayons, pens/pencils
★   scissors and glue
★   sheets of white paper and coloured paper
★   coloured tissue paper / alphabet letters
★   plastic pockets or wallets
★   stickers and stamps

Arranging your scrapbook
1. Collect photographs that show you, your family, your friends, where you live, your school and places you have visited — also photos of things that interest you, from magazines and newspapers, for example.
2. Arrange these pictures in different categories: you; your family; grandparents; friends; your home; your school; pets; special occasions, such as birthdays or first day at school; places you have visited; funny snapshots. Make sure to have a category called 'Miscellaneous'.
3. Use the dividers to make separate sections for each category.
4. With your alphabet letters, name each category. You may prefer to draw the names using special block letters and then colour them in.
5. Attach the photos to the white or coloured pages. Write the date, title and a description for each picture. Decorate with the tissue paper.
6. Place each completed page inside a plastic wallet or pocket and attach it within the correct category inside the ring binder.
7. The stickers and stamps will add extra colour to each display page.
8. Remember to place a few extra blank pages in each category to allow for new photos to be included.

Display
To keep your Life Scrapbook up to date, add new material to each section as time goes by.

Examine the Instructions

Read the instructions and answer the following.

① What is the purpose of making different categories in the scrapbook?

_____

_____

② Why is a ring binder suitable for putting a scrapbook together?

_____

_____

③ What is the reason for using plastic pockets or wallets?

_____

_____

④ In which category would you place the following photographs?

(a) You washing your pet dog, Rufus, in the garden _____

(b) You at the Christmas pantomime _____

(c) Grandad Jim on his bicycle _____

(d) On the beach in Majorca _____

(e) Your parents holding you when you were born _____

⑤ Why should extra blank pages be placed in each section in the ring binder?

_____

_____

⑥ What is the purpose of writing about each photograph and picture?

_____

_____

⑦ What could you put in the section called 'Miscellaneous'?

_____

_____

⑧ Do you think that a life scrapbook is a good idea? _____ Say why.

_____

_____

_____

Write Instructions for a Scrapbook

Now you can write instructions to make a different type of scrapbook, e.g. for sports, for holidays or for fashion. Use the frame to help you.

Making a _____

Description

_____

Aim

_____

Materials   **Illustration**

_____

_____

_____

_____

_____

_____

Instructions

_____

_____

_____

_____

_____

_____

_____

_____

_____

_____

_____

_____

_____

Revise and check this first draft. Write the final draft in your copy or on your computer. Include diagrams or pictures.

Explanation Writing

We write explanations to explain to the reader

★ **how** things occur.
★ **why** things are or happen.
★ **how** things operate or work.

Explanation writing is found in

★ Non-fiction books
★ Handbooks and technical manuals
★ Science books
★ Social and Environmental Studies books
★ Encyclopaedias
★ Internet web pages

When you write an explanation, it helps to

★ press your curiosity button!
★ brainstorm what you already know about the topic.
★ ask yourself when, where, how, why questions to find out more.
★ research – be a detective!
★ organise your information, using the writing frame.

How Does the Brain Work?

Talk about the diagram and read the explanation.

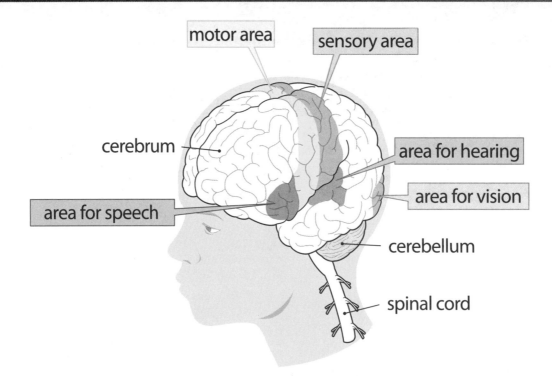

The brain is a living **organ** inside your head, which controls your whole body. It keeps all parts of the body working and is responsible for thoughts, feelings and memory. You also use the brain to make sense of the things you experience.

The brain fits snugly inside a hard bony case called the **skull**. The skull protects the brain, which itself looks like a mass of grey, wrinkled and wobbly jelly. Taking up about half of the space inside the head, an adult's brain weighs about 1.4 kilograms.

The human brain is divided into many different areas, which control the things you do, say, hear, feel, think and see (see diagram). The largest part of the brain is called the cerebrum, which has two sides. The right side of the brain controls the left side of the body and the left side of the brain controls the right side of the body. It has also been discovered that each side of the brain looks after different skills and activities. The right side controls artistic talent and imagination, while the left is responsible for working things out like mathematical problems and **logical** thinking. Below the cerebrum lies the cerebellum, which helps you to balance and co-ordinate your movements.

The brain operates like a computer inside your head. It is linked to the body by the **spinal cord** and **nerves.** Your nerves are like long, thin wires that run all over the body. These operate like telephone wires, sending information to and from the brain in the form of tiny electrical currents. In the human body, there are 100 million nerves. Some carry messages from your five senses to the brain, while others bring instructions from the brain to your muscles. Since the brain acts like the control centre of the body, its job is to keep track of and to make sense of all this information.

The brain is both a fascinating and a truly amazing organ. About the size of two fists, it works automatically day and night and keeps the body ticking over even when you are fast asleep. It controls many things like breathing and sends signals to the nerves at speeds of up to 400 km per hour!

Examine This Explanation

Examine the explanation carefully and answer the following.

① Underline the sentence which explains what a brain is.

② Use your dictionary to explain the words in bold type.

organ _____

skull _____

logical _____

spinal cord _____

nerves _____

③ Explain what facts you have understood from this explanation about the human brain, by answering the following.

(a) **When** do you use it? _____

_____

(b) **Where** is it? _____

(c) **What** does it look like? _____

(d) **Why** do we need it? _____

_____

(e) **How** does it work? _____

_____

_____

④ What information about the brain did you find most interesting?

_____

_____

_____

⑤ Why, do you think, is the brain compared to a computer?

_____

_____

_____

Follow-up Activity

Sometimes the body reacts without waiting for a message from the brain. This is called a reflex action. To observe a reflex action, sit with your legs crossed and ask a friend to tap gently below your kneecap. When the right spot is tapped, your foot will jerk up!

Plan an Explanation

Follow these steps to plan an explanation on the topic 'Why Do Humans Have Skin?' Use the frames to help you.

(A) Make notes:

1) What do I already know about the topic?

My ideas

_____

_____

_____

2) Research the topic. Discuss it and brainstorm in class.

Class research

_____

_____

_____

_____

(B) Use the headings in this plan to organise your thoughts and write information in each section of the explanation frame.

Title: I am going to explain why humans have skin.

Definition: What is skin? _____

_____

Cause and effect: The **when**, **why**, **where** and **how** of human skin...

_____

_____

_____

_____

_____

_____

What else do I know? Any other interesting facts?

_____

_____

_____

_____

Revise and check this first draft. Write the final draft in your copy or on your computer. Use drawings and/or diagrams to help you.

Grammar and Punctuation (13)

Pronouns

(A) Only one of the following is the correct definition of a pronoun. Write the correct one.

1) a word that tells us more about a verb
2) an action word
3) a word used instead of a noun
4) the name of a person, animal, place or thing
5) a describing word

A pronoun is_____

(B) Write ten more pronouns.

us   they   _____ _____ _____ _____

_____ _____ _____ _____ _____ _____

(C) Write the correct pronoun in each of the following sentences.

1) It is time for _____ (I, me) to go to bed.

2) My friend and _____ (I, me) went for a walk.

3) She invited Ann and _____ (I, me) to the party.

4) Robert and _____ (I, me) got a present.

(D) What noun is replaced by the pronoun **It** in the following sentences from the explanation? _____

The brain operates like a computer inside your head. It is linked to the body by the spinal cord and nerves.

(E) Underline the pronouns in the following extracts from the explanation. In your copy, write another sentence for each one.

The brain is a living organ inside your head, which controls your whole body. It keeps all parts of the body working and is responsible for thoughts, feelings and memory. You also use the brain to make sense of the things you experience.

These operate like telephone wires, sending….

(F) Write the sentence from the explanation that contains the pronouns 'some', 'your' and 'others'.

_____

_____

Why Do Plants Need Sunlight?

Talk about the diagrams below and read the explanation.

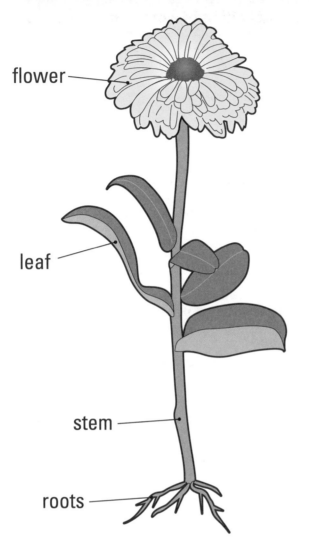

flower

leaf

stem

roots

Light is a form of **energy**. Sunlight is energy which comes directly from the sun. Plants use the energy in sunlight to make food for themselves in their leaves.

Plants make food by turning light from the sun into food **chemicals** in their leaves. The name given to this process is photosynthesis, which means 'building with light'. A leaf is designed to do this job efficiently. Generally broad and flat, leaves act as green **solar panels** to **absorb** as much sunlight as possible.

Each leaf contains a green substance called **chlorophyll**, which gives the leaf its colour and can capture the energy in sunlight.

Once captured, the sunlight energy can make food. To do this, the leaf also needs water and a chemical called **carbon dioxide**. Water comes from the soil and is carried up to the leaf from the roots through the stem of the plant. Carbon dioxide, a gas found in air, is taken into the leaf through tiny holes on its underside called stomata. The energy stored in the leaf is then used to turn the water and carbon dioxide into **glucose**, a sugary food the plant can feed on. Oxygen and water are produced too and these pass out through the stomata and into the air.

A leaf is really a food-producing factory and all parts of the plant work together to help it to do its very important job. The sugary food that is made in the leaves is carried, in a liquid called sap, to all the other parts of the plant.

No wonder then that flowers and plants seem to turn to face the sun as it moves across the sky and that most plants on Earth have green leaves and stems!

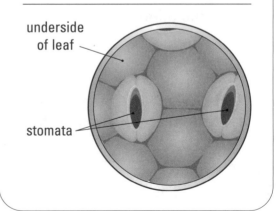

The underside of a leaf as seen through a microscope.

underside of leaf

stomata

Examine this Explanation

Examine the explanation carefully and answer the following.

① Underline the sentence(s) which explain(s) what the word sunlight means.

② Use your dictionary to explain the highlighted words in the explanation.

energy _____

chemicals _____

solar panels _____

absorb _____

chlorophyll _____

carbon dioxide _____

glucose _____

③ Explain what you have understood from this description of photosynthesis, by answering the following.

(a) It happens **where**?_____

(b) **Why** here? _____

_____

(c) **What** else is needed?_____

_____

(d) **How** does it happen?_____

_____

④ What new information did you find most interesting in this explanation?

_____

_____

⑤ What do you think would happen to a plant that was placed in darkness for a week or two? _____

What experiment would you do to test this?

_____

_____

_____

Follow-up Activity

Discuss and research why trees are sometimes called 'the lungs of the planet'.

Plan an Explanation

Follow these steps to plan an explanation on the topic 'Why Do We Need Plants?' Use the frames to help you.

(A) Make notes:

1) What do I already know about the topic?

My ideas

_____

_____

_____

2) Research the topic. Discuss it and brainstorm in class.

Class research

_____

_____

_____

(B) Use the headings in this plan to organise your thoughts and write information in each section of the explanation frame.

Title: I am going to explain why we need plants.

Definition: What is a plant? _____

_____

Cause and effect: The **when**, **why**, **where** and **how** of plants and their uses…

_____

_____

_____

_____

_____

What else do I know? Any other interesting facts?

_____

_____

_____

_____

Revise and check this first draft. Write the final draft in your copy or on your computer. Use drawings and/or diagrams to help you.

Grammar and Punctuation (14)

Revision

(A) Write one fact that you know about each of the following and share your answers with your group or class.

★ the sentence

_____

★ capital letters

_____

★ full stops

_____

★ the comma

_____

★ the question mark

_____

★ the apostrophe

_____

★ quotation marks / speech marks

_____

(B) Write four examples of each of the following parts of speech.

★ nouns	_____	_____	_____	_____
★ pronouns	_____	_____	_____	_____
★ adjectives	_____	_____	_____	_____
★ verbs	_____	_____	_____	_____
★ adverbs	_____	_____	_____	_____
★ prepositions	_____	_____	_____	_____
★ conjunctions	_____	_____	_____	_____

(C) Spot the deliberate mistakes in spelling and punctuation in this extract. Mark the mistakes and then write the extract correctly in your copy.

the old man drew close to the gate and swung down his sack when he confronted jody his lips flutered a little and a soft empersonal voice came from between them do you live here jody was imbarrassed he turned and looked at the house and he turned back and looked towards the barn where his father and billy buck were Yes he said when no help came form either direction I have come back the old man said I am gitano, and I have come back.

When you are finished, check your work with the last paragraphs on page 30.

How Does a Car Engine Work?

The car, the most popular kind of **transport** in the world, is a road **vehicle** with four wheels and an engine. An engine is a machine which converts energy into mechanical power or movement. Most cars have engines that are powered by **petrol** or gasoline.

Engines are far more powerful than muscles so machines can move much faster than legs. On a motorway, a car can travel at a speed of up to 120 kilometres an hour. The driving force under the bonnet of each car is an internal combustion engine. The engine is a *combustion* engine because it burns or combusts fuel. It is an *internal* combustion engine because the fuel burns inside the engine's cylinder.

Cars need petrol like humans need food. They get the energy to move by burning petrol inside their engines. Petrol, a **fossil fuel**, has energy locked inside it and this energy is set free inside the car engine and it is used to turn the car wheels.

How exactly is this energy released? Petrol is kept in a tank and is pumped along a pipe to the engine. A mixture of air and petrol comes into a cylinder in the engine and a piston squeezes the mixed-up air and petrol into a small space at the top of the cylinder (see diagram). Then an electric spark, caused by turning the ignition key, jumps from a spark plug which is plugged into the top of the cylinder. This causes the petrol and air to explode, pushing the piston back down again. These continuous explosions make the piston move up and down in the cylinder. The up-and-down motion of the piston causes the crankshaft to spin and this turns the wheels round and round. **Emissions** from the burning petrol are pushed out of the engine through the exhaust pipe.

Since burning fossil fuels produces **fumes**, which pollute the environment, the search is on to find another more environmentally friendly means of powering cars. Some modern cars do not burn petrol but use energy from the sun and other sources like electricity, stored in a battery. Cars that run on electricity, for example, are both cleaner and quieter. In fact, the first car to go faster than 100 kilometres an hour was battery-powered. It was called 'La Jamais Contente' and it broke the record over 100 years ago, in 1899!

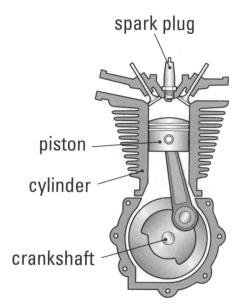

spark plug

piston

cylinder

crankshaft

Examine this Explanation

Examine the explanation carefully and answer the following.

1. Underline the sentences which explain (a) what a car is and (b) what an engine is.

2. Explain the highlighted words from the passage, using a dictionary.

   transport _____

   vehicle _____

   petrol _____

   fossil fuel _____

   emissions _____

   fumes _____

3. Write one fact from the explanation which proves that engines are more powerful than muscles. Write another example of your own.

   _____

   _____

   _____

4. In the explanation find and write another word for each of the following.

   petrol _____   combust _____

   internal _____   set free _____

5. Write five sentences to explain how a car engine works.

   First _____

   Then _____

   This causes _____

   The explosion forces _____

   Because of this _____

6. What new and interesting fact have you learned about car engines?

   _____

   _____

   _____

Follow-up Activity

With your teacher or guardian, browse the website at www.sei.ie to explore alternative forms of energy to fossil fuels.

Plan an Explanation

Follow these steps to plan an explanation on the topic 'How Does an Aeroplane Fly?' Use the writing frames to help you.

(A) **Make notes:**

1) What do I already know about the topic?

My ideas

_____

_____

_____

2) Research the topic. Discuss it and brainstorm in class.

Class research

_____

_____

_____

(B) **Use the headings in this plan to organise your thoughts and write information in each section of the explanation frame.**

Title: I am going to explain how an aeroplane flies.

Definition: What is an aeroplane? _____

_____

Cause and effect: The **how**, **why**, **where** and **when** of engine-powered flight...

_____

_____

_____

_____

_____

_____

_____

What else do I know? Any other interesting facts?

_____

_____

_____

Revise and check this first draft. Write the final draft in your copy or on your computer. Use drawings and/or diagrams to help you.

Teacher's Notes

Reasons to Write introduces children to the many **purposes** for which we write and to the **audiences** for whom we write. The **genres** examined and explored in this book are

- *Recount Writing*
- *Persuasive Writing*
- *Report Writing*
- *Explanation Writing*
- *Procedural Writing*
- *Narrative Writing*
- *Poetry Writing*

In each case, the children are given the opportunity to

- **read** a sample of the particular form of writing as modelled.
- **examine** its content and analyse its structure.
- **write** within the genre.

It is important to remember that there can be overlap between the various genres. For example, recount writing involves narrative. Procedural and report writing often include explanation. Poetry can be persuasive. In addition, the same topic can be treated in different ways and from a number of perspectives. For example, it is possible to

- *write a story* about an adventure in a hot-air balloon.
- *explain* how a balloon works.
- *recount* an experience in a balloon.
- *write a report* describing hot-air balloons.
- *persuade* someone to take a trip in a balloon.
- *show procedures* for making a model of a balloon.
- *write a poem* about a balloon.

Reasons to Write demonstrates how writing is used across all areas of the curriculum. The wide range of writing topics includes aspects of Science, Geography, History, SPHE, Music, P.E., Visual Arts and Drama. This cross-curricular approach demonstrates the various forms and functions of writing and is thus essential to the development of literacy.

Grammar pages are included to highlight aspects of grammar and punctuation, to heighten children's awareness and to develop the necessary writing skills. Since examples are based on the texts, it is an opportunity to learn about grammar in context and affords opportunities for immediate application.

Using this book to introduce a genre of writing to your class

1. **Decide** which genre you wish to focus on. There is no particular order recommended although recount writing may be the type of writing with which children are most familiar and is the one which is closest to their own experience.

2. **Devote** five to six weeks to the exploration of each genre.

3. **Introduce** the genre to the class by **discussing** the information given on the title page for the section you are studying. Children then **read** a sample of the particular form of writing, **examine** the text, **plan** their own writing and use **writing frames** to help them to **compose a first draft**.

4. **Give guidance** to the children regarding the specific features you wish to focus on during drafting and editing.

5. **Encourage** children to research and write at a level which suits their individual learning style and ability.

6. **Publish** and **display** the children's finished work in a variety of ways.

7. **Explore** the **grammar** and **punctuation** as presented, making sure to provide further practice with your own follow-up material.

8. **Ensure** that class and group **discussion feature** at all stages of the writing process.

The Writing Process

Regardless of the genre chosen, it is important that we guide children through the writing process in a step-by-step way.

This book is formulated to help you to follow these essential steps with your class.

- **Discussion and planning**
- **Decision making**
- **Drafting**
- **Editing**
- **Re-drafting**
- **Presentation and publication**
- **Feedback**
- **Reflection**

Each of these steps forms a vital part of learning to write, and children need to be supported at each stage.

Discussion and planning: This involves class discussions and debate, choosing topics, brainstorming, prioritising, organising of information and drawing flow charts and diagrams.

Decision making: Decide on the form of writing to be approached, the purpose of the writing, the audience for whom it is intended, the subject of the text, and how the final work will be presented.

Drafting: This enables children the freedom to write unselfconsciously, knowing that they will have the opportunity later to edit and re-draft.